The Little Book of
LIMERICKS

The Little Book of
LIMERICKS

BY H. I. BROCK, 1876 - 1961, comp.

Granger Index Reprint Series

 BOOKS FOR LIBRARIES PRESS
FREEPORT, NEW YORK

Acknowledgement To Original Edition

"The Lady from Pompton Lakes," "The
Maiden in Harrison," "The Peeping Tom of
Fort Lee," and "The Clergyman from Dumont" quoted from *Spilt Milk,* Copyright
1929, 1942 by Morris Bishop, are here re-
printed through the courtesy of G. P. Put-
nam's Sons.

STANDARD BOOK NUMBER:
8369-6053-X

To Lester Markel
Sunday Editor of *The New York Times*

The idea of this collection of limericks fit to print was
yours; the beginning was in the pages of the *Times
Magazine*. It is only fair, therefore, that you should accept the consequences—and the grateful acknowledgments of the compiler—and stand godfather to this
little book.

H. I. B.

Table of Organization

The Little Book of
LIMERICKS

Introduction

NOBODY knows, for sure, when the tricky and often impudent five-line verse form, called the limerick, was invented, or who was the inventor. But this much is certain. Edward Lear gave the skittish rhythmical contrivance the vogue which has made it one of the favorite playthings, alike of metrical experts and unterrified amateurs, the whetstone upon which scholars have sharpened the knives of their wit and made their learning accomplice before the fact.

Lear wrote his limericks for children, and children love nonsense. He was then a young artist and was employed making careful pictures of birds and beasts for a monumental catalogue of the private menagerie of the thirteenth Earl of Derby. In Lear's own words, Knowsley Hall, the Earl's seat, "Abounded in children

3

and mirth." In his spare time the bird-painter began
to draw pictures and write accompanying nonsense
verses to amuse the juvenile crew. Again in his own
words, "uproarious delight" greeted "the appearance
of every new absurdity." Somebody had told him that
the lines beginning, "There was an old man of Tobago"
made a handy model for his purpose. Thus the limerick
became his chosen instrument.

Obviously, "The Old Man of Tobago" was already in
circulation. So Lear did not invent the limerick—
though Mr. Punch's learned clerk, E. V. Knox has sug-
gested that the tag might be a corruption of "Learick"
—and nobody has been able to find more than a tenu-
ous link between the limerick as a verse form and the
Irish city and county of that name.

Of that more later, perhaps. Anyhow, just one hundred and one years ago a collection of these verses and
pictures was published. It was called "The Book of
Nonsense." And as the saying is, Lear waked up to find
himself famous. Every one of the hundred-odd verses
was a limerick. And wherever it had started and whatever had been its previous history, the limerick was
launched upon its career.

As for Lear, his limericks, written for children, were

nursery-clean. In fact, they gave him such a reputation as a pure young man that he was presently engaged as Queen Victoria's drawing master. In limerick form, what happened has been described this way:

> There once was an artist named Lear
> Who wrote verses to make children cheer.
>   Though they never made sense,
>   Their success was immense;
> And the Queen thought that Lear was a dear.

(However, they do say the nursery-rhymer, translated to Buckingham Palace, would, in Her Majesty's presence, stand in front of the Royal fire—which was "contrary to etiquette.")

Since then, the limerick has fallen into the hands of persons more intent on diverting grown-ups bored with being sensible than on amusing small fry fed up with doing lessons. A dash of impropriety gave zest to literary diet even in Queen Victoria's glorious days. Indeed, the bounds of propriety imposed by the social code of those days—for mixed parties—was an incitement to relaxation when the parties weren't mixed.

Moreover, "a little nonsense now and then is relished by the wisest men."

Limericks had arrived in a book of nonsense. The transition is easy from nonsense to nonconformity. Obedience to the rules limiting freedom of speech in polite circles certainly came under the heading of conformity. Consequently, limericks tended to be bawdy. One limerick leads to another; competition is invited. The nonsense verse-form promoted by that particularly pure young man lends itself readily to what we may call, most politely, poetic license. Limericks got bawdier and bawdier.

With the rise of democracy and the extension of the suffrage to the under-privileged of both sexes—or, if you please, the over-privileged of one of them—manners have become freer, language less considerately toned to what Jane Austen calls the "delicacy of the elegant female." In time the gap between the smoking room and the drawing room has narrowed until there is just as much smoke in one as in the other, with the ladies doing at least their share of the smoking. The cocktail lounge has tended to replace both smoking room and drawing room—whether the scene is a public place or a private house—and this has gone so far that it is a question whether barroom ways have not become the common denominator of social behavior. Restraining influences have steadily diminished.

Don Marquis, who made writing limericks a liberal art, a generation ago set up a market-price classification about like this:

Limericks that can be told in the presence of ladies—$1
Limericks that can be told in the presence of the clergy—$2
Limericks   —$10

That classification is out on two counts. And today it is not easy to draw the line between "clean" limericks and the other kind. That is a difficulty we face in making this selection. We propose to lean a bit backward in order not to offend the fastidious or invite conscientious objectors to punitive action as *censores morum*. If, to the more liberal, the absence of four-letter words gives a flat taste to the dish, we'd like to point out—with due diffidence—that the real trick in the confection called the limerick is a neat combination of metrical perfection, verbal felicity, and a quick turn of wit. Without these three, the bawdiest limerick is stale and unprofitable.

Personally, after years of exposure to limericks not fit to print in a family newspaper or in a volume *virginibus puerisque,* we have been surprised at the number of limericks which meet the requirements above noted and, at the same time, *are* fit to print. Our aim, then, is to conform to the canon imposed on talk at The Players by Oliver Herford, a master hand who could and did play limericks all across the board. "Not a word," said Oliver, "that's profane or obscene." And so say we, at least by modern standards. We might add that many of the inventions that come under the wire have more highly flavored versions; and perhaps some of our readers can supply the missing words.

As to the age of the limerick, a keen-nosed sleuth in the field has discovered one in the works of William Shakespeare (We'll give it to you later). And a scholar, F. A. Wright, has been able to translate into a perfectly good limerick—and that without sacrifice of sense or blunting the point of the original—one of the snatches of drinking songs with which Aristophanes has enlivened the last part of "The Wasps."

The inventor of musical comedy did not have the

benefit—or, if you are a disciple of the modern school of free verse, the handicap—of rhyme. The Greeks didn't use rhyme. Consequently they didn't have limericks in our form. But, if you are interested in purely technical matters, their word for satiric verse was "anapesta"—to employ the Latinized form of the word. Freely translated from the Greek, that says "back kick."

The essence of the limerick's performance is just that. Moreover, orthodox limericks are written in anapestic rhythm. If you are a little more curious and do not happen to know all about such things, the metrical trick involved is the reverse—or counter stroke—of the dactyl—two short syllables and one long (or accented) syllable, in place of a long and two shorts following. Try it on our limericks and you can determine the orthodoxy of any one of them.

E. V. Knox tells us, in the Fourteenth Edition of the Encyclopaedia Britannica, that Langford Reed is the collector of limericks who has toiled most manfully to clear up the mystery of the creature's pre-Learian past. Reed says that this peculiar verse form was brought to us from France by way of Ireland. The carriers were the returned veterans of the Irish Brigade—an outfit which had been serving with the French Army for a

hundred years or ever since 1691, when Patrick Sars-
field, after surrendering Limerick to King William's
men, took a lot of the stout fellows who had been fight-
ing for King James over the water to fight for Louis
XIV. Thus the limerick came to Limerick.

In order to plant the limerick in France at that date,
Reed cites from Boswell's *Johnson* an epigram lifted
from *Menagiana* of 1716 about a young lady who came
to a masquerade dressed as a Jesuit. It is a limerick
without doubt, and gains contemporary flavor from the
fact that it gets its point from the active debate then
going on between the followers of Miguel de Molinos
and those of the anti-Jesuit Cornelius Jensen. The essence of it is that the lady who is parading as an arch
conservative is a liberal, and thus improperly dressed.

> On s'étonne ici que Caliste
> Ait pris l'habit de Moliniste,
>   Puisque cette jeune beauté
>   Ote á chacun sa liberté
> N'est ce pas une Janseniste?

In the same connection, Reed quotes also a French
version of "Dickory, Dickory, Dock, The Mouse Ran
up the Clock." It goes like this:

Digerie, digerie, doge
La souris ascend l'horloge,
  L'horloge frappe,,
  La souris s'échappe,
Digerie, digerie, doge.

This, certainly, is not an orthodox limerick. In Knox's
opinion it permits in the verse form a "license almost
as wide as that latterly attained in morals."

If this attempt to tie the limerick to the Irish city of
the same name seems more contrived than convincing,
there is another story which creates an association at
least. As told in responsible reference books, it is this:
Limericks used to be sung at convivial gatherings as
impromptus, and they were accompanied by an invar-
iable chorus, as follows:

Won't you come up, come up,
Won't you come up, I say,
Won't you come up, come all the way up,
Come all the way up to Limerick?

On the ground that nothing in this chorus fits into
the meter or pattern of the limerick, Knox and other
eminent authorities refuse to accept this explanation.

However, Rodman Gilder (a Harvard man) tells us
that limericks were sung in his recollection and with
this chorus. And, for what it is worth, there are wit-
nesses to prove that at least one limerick was composed
in Limerick—the composer, Archibald MacLeish, and
the date not more than two years back.

We have mentioned already that a limerick has been
found in Shakespeare. It is in a drinking song, like the
one manipulated out of Aristophanes. Leonard Bacon
(a Yale man, believe it or not) and one of our own
learned clerks who is as ready as Punch's own Mr.
Knox at putting the muse of poetry into motley, has
pointed out that we can find half a dozen or so in the
Grosvenor Gallery song in Sir W. S. Gilbert's *Patience.*
Take for example the last five lines of the first stanza,
delivered by Bunthorne:

> I shall, with cultured taste,
> Distinguish gems from paste.
>   And "High diddle, diddle"
>   Will rank as an idyll
> If I pronounce it chaste.

Of course it isn't orthodox—the anapests are entirely
missing in the three long lines. Sir William, in Bacon's

words, has preferred to use as his vehicle a "sort of Crosley convertible."

Wherever the limerick came from—whether it began as a French *fal-lal* fetched over to us through Ireland by licentious soldiery, or whatever—nothing human is excluded from its range. In politics, divinity, philosophy, philology, sociology, zoology; in botany, Latinity, relativity, revelry, and ribaldry; it is equally at home. Geography is its happy hunting ground. Matters vegetable, animal, and mineral are grist to its mill. Love, sacred and profane, is fair game. Bishops and tabby cats are equal targets.

And the follies, foibles, fortunes, failures and fallacies to which our mortal flesh is heir, from the cradle to the grave, are the stuff to which its antics give the *coup de pied.*

Language, ancient and modern, is its tool and its toy; nor all their wisdom nor all their wit can put a bridle on the imp who grins and gambols within the tight limits of the five-barred cage that contains him.

"The spirit," as the Young Man with the Cream Tarts said to Prince Florizel of Bohemia, "the spirit, Sir, is one of mockery."

Touching the form, we give you the doctor's prescription: ℞ (O Jupiter aid us) Five anapestic lines, of which one, two, and five are of three feet and rhyme; and three and four are of two feet and rhyme. Lear used a "lazy" last line repeating the first with a changed word or two but almost always ending with the rhyme word of the first. Later practitioners make a new last line the proof of the pudding.

Modestly marked anonymous in David McCord's *Pocket Book of Humorous Verse* is this explanation in terms of aerodynamical design of what gives the limerick its lift.

> Well, it's partly the shape of the thing
> That gives the old limerick wing;
>   These accordion pleats,
>   Full of airy conceits,
> Take it up like a kite on a string.

If you find that not many of these limericks are tagged with an author's name, please remember—even if you are the author—that the limerick has wings and does not stay put on the printed page. Once airborne by word of mouth, it is on its own; and the more it gets carried around without credit, the greater the compli-

ment to the author. *Vox populi* has given his work the
Order of Merit.

Besides, many limericks, before they get into print
have been hammered into shape by a choice group of
wits in congress assembled under the sign, IN VINO
VERITAS—make it bourbon or scotch, if you prefer.
And the author who signs on the printed page does
not know himself who is the father of the child. So
pardon us, so pardon us, if we too seldom date and
sign.[1]

The fact remains that in this collection of many inventions the credit for every limerick belongs to the
person—named or unnamed—who invented it; and
that the collector, who has made the assembly a labor
of love, hereby makes grateful acknowledgment to
each and every one of them. Much of what has come
into the net has got there by word of mouth. Most of
what came by way of the printed word belongs to the
group which a discriminating public would never for-
give any collector of limericks for omitting.

Again: Putting limericks in order is something like
making close-order drill take with the Air Corps. Hav-
ing wings, limericks, also, are allergic to discipline. If

you put 'em in categories they will not stay there. Nevertheless, the design of this book calls for the appearance, at least, of orderly arrangement. We have done what we could about it, and put Lear's Own at the head of the procession.

H. I. B.

Learicks—or Lazy-Liners
(Edward Lear's Own)

There was an old man with a beard,
Who said, "It is just as I feared!
  Two Owls and a Hen,
  Four Larks and a Wren
Have all built their nests in my beard."

There was an old man in a tree
Who was horribly bored by a bee,
   When they said, "Does it buzz?
   He replied, "Yes, it does,
It's a regular brute of a bee." [2]

There was an old person of Ware
Who rode on the back of a bear;
   When they asked, "Does it trot?"
   He said, "Certainly not,
It's a Moppsikon, Floppsikon Bear."

There was an old man of Thermopylæ
Who never did anything properly;
But they said, "If you choose
To boil eggs in your shoes,
You cannot remain in Thermopylæ."

There was an old man who supposed
That the street door was partially closed.
But some very large rats
Ate his coats and his hats
While the futile old gentleman dozed.[8]

There was a young girl of Majorca
Whose Aunt was a very fast walker.
   She walked sixty miles
   And leaped fifteen stiles,
Which astonished that girl from Majorca.

There was an old person of Anerly
Whose conduct was strange and unmannerly
   He rushed down the Strand
   With a pig in each hand,
But returned in the evening to Anerly.

There was an old man of Vesuvius
Who studied the works of Vitruvius;
  When flames burnt his book,
  To drinking he took,
That morbid old man of Vesuvius.

There was an Old Man of the Coast,
Who placidly sat on a Post;
  But when it was cold,
  He relinquished his hold,
And called for some Hot Buttered Toast.

There was an Old Man with a beard,
Who sat on a horse when he reared:
   But they said, "Never mind!
   You will fall off behind,
You propitious Old Man with a beard."

Light Brigade—WAC

There was a trim maiden named Wood
Who only did things that she should,
  Till she reasoned one day—
  "If I really want play,
'Tis time I did things which I could."
                    William A. Lockwood

Said a girl from beyond Pompton Lakes,
"I do make the most stupid mistakes,
   Now the car's in the hall;
   It went right through the wall,
When I mixed up the gas and the brakes.
                         Morris Bishop

There was a young lady of Lynn
Who was deep in original sin;
   When they said, "Do be good!"
   She said, "Would, if I could."
And straightway went at it ag'in.

There was a young lady from Joppa
Whose friends all decided to drop her:
   She went with a friend
   On a trip to Ostend—
And the rest of the story's improper.

A young man on a journey had met her,
And tried just his hardest to get her,
   He knelt at her feet—
   Said: "I'd die for you, sweet,"
And she cruelly told him he'd better.

There's a vaporish maiden in Harrison
Who longed for the love of a Saracen.
  But she had to confine her
  Intent to a Shriner,
Who suffers, I fear, by comparison.
                                    Morris Bishop

The Captains and the Kings
(or Lives of Great Men All Remind Us)

Said Nero to one of his train,
"These Christians will surely refrain,
    Encased as they are
    In coatings of tar,
From burning my city again."

There was a young man of Madrid
Who fancied that he was the Cid:
    When they asked of him "Why?"
    He could only reply
That he didn't know why, but he did.

◇—◇—◇

I saw Nelson at the Battle of the Nile,
And did the bullets whistle—I should smile!
    And when Pharaoh hit the King
    With a cutlass of the wing,
I was lying at the bottom of the pile.[4]

◇—◇—◇

Mussolini's pet Marshal, Graziani
Marched his troops into Sidi Barrani,
  But Sir Arichibald Wavell
  Kicked him once in the navel
And twenty-five times in the fanny.

                T. R. Ybarra

U. S. S. R.

A canny old codger at Yalta
Sent two statesmen back home, and at Malta,
   They talked quite a spell,
   And then they said, "Hell,
He's just like rock of Gibraltar."

Should a plan we suggest, just that minute,
The Muscovite lines up agin it.
   He won't play at all
    'Less we give him the ball,
And he's got the game fixed so he'll win it.
                      R. K. B.

Bishops and Tabby Cats

And those two young ladies of Birmingham,
Have you heard the sad story concerning 'em?
 They stuck needles and pins
 In the knees and the shins
Of the Bishop while he was confirming 'em.

Cleopatra, who thought they maligned her,
Resolved to reform and be kinder:
  "If, when pettish," she said,
  "I should knock off your head,
Won't you give me a gentle reminder?"

There was a young man who was bitten
By twenty-two cats and a kitten;
  Sighed he, "It is clear
  My finish is near;
No matter; I'll die like a Briton."

Walter Parke

There was an old stupid who wrote
The verses above that we quote;
His want of all sense
Was something immense,
Which made him a person of note.

Walter Parke

Summer Hotels

These places abound in the old,
Who do nothing but quibble and scold,
    Discussing their tumors
    And stock-market rumors.
They are tangibly covered with mold.
              George Libaire

There was a young man at St. Kitts
Who was very much troubled with fits;
    An eclipse of the moon
    Threw him into a swoon,
When he tumbled and broke all to bits.

Dealers in Magic and Spells

A beautiful lady named Psyche
Is loved by a fellow named Yche.
  One thing about Ych
  The lady can't lych
Is his beard, which is dreadfully spyche.

The life boat that's kept at Torquay
Is intended to float on the suay;
   The crew and the coxswain
   Are sturdy as oxswain
And as smart and as brave as can buay.

Miss Minnie McFinney of Butte
Fed always, and only, on frutte.
   Said she: "Let the coarse
   Eat of beef and of horse,
I'm a peach, and that's all there is tutte."
                              Carolyn Wells

There was a young maiden, a Sioux,
As tempting as fresh honeydioux.
　　She displayed her cute knees
　　As she strolled past tepees,
And the braves, they all hollared "Wioux-Wioux!"

There was a young curate of Salisbury
Whose manners were most Halisbury-Scalisbury.
　　He wandered 'round Hampshire
　　Without any pampshire,
Till the vicar compelled him to Walmisbury.[5]

George Libaire

An amorous M. A.
Said of Cupid, the C. D.
  "From their prodigal use,
  He is, I deduce,
The John Jacob H." [6]

College of Physicians and Surgeons

There once were some learned MD's
Who captured some germs of disease,
  And infected a train,
  Which, without causing pain,
Allowed one to catch it with ease.

Oliver Herford

There was a faith healer of Deal
Who said, "Although pain is not real,
   When I sit on a pin
   And it punctures my skin,
I dislike what I fancy I feel."

No matter how grouchy you're feeling,
You will find the smile more or less healing.
   It grows in a wreath
   All around the front teeth,
Thus preserving the face from congealing.

A man to whom illness was chronic,
When told that he needed a tonic,
   Said, "Oh, Doctor, dear,
   Won't you, please, make it beer?"
"No, no," said the Doc, "that's Teutonic."

There was an Old Man of Tobago
Who lived on rice, gruel and sago:
   Till, much to his bliss,
   His physician said this:
"To a leg, Sir, of mutton you may go."

There was an old man of Tarentum
Who gnashed his false teeth till he bent 'em.
  When they asked him the cost
  Of what he had lost,
He replied, "I can't say, for I rent 'em."

Subject: Matrimony

There was a young man of Fort Blainy
Who proposed to his typist, named Janey;
   When his friends said, "Oh, dear!
   She's so old and so queer,"
He replied, "But the day was so rainy."

There was a young fellow from Fife
Who had a big row with his wife.
   He lost half his nose,
   Two-thirds of his toes,
One ear, seven teeth—and his life.
               T. R. Ybarra

There was a young fellow of Lyme
Who lived with three wives at a time.
   When they asked: "Why the third?"
   He replied: "One's absurd.
And bigamy, Sir, is a crime.'

There was a young fellow named Dice
Who remarked, "They say bigamy's nice.
    Even two are a bore,
    I'd prefer three or four,
For the plural of spouse, it is spice."

Wine and Food Society

An epicure dining at Crewe,
Found quite a large mouse in his stew.
  Said the waiter, "Don't shout,
  And wave it about,
Or the rest will be wanting some, too." [7]

There was a young lady of Kent
Who said that she knew what it meant
    When men asked her to dine,
    Gave her cocktails and wine:
She knew what it meant—but she went.[8]

There was a young person named Tate
Who went out to dine at 8:8;
    But I will not relate
    What that person named Tate
And his tête-à-tête ate at 8:8.

There was a fair maid from Decatur
Who was known as red-hot potato.
   To the jungle she went,
   On mission work bent,
Where a dozen fat savages ate her.

There once was a bonnie Scotch laddie,
Who said, as he put on his plaidie:
   "I've just had a dish
   O' unco' guid fish."
What had 'e had? Had 'e had haddie?

A half baked potato, named Sue,
Was withdrawn to thicken a stew.
  She reluctantly cried,
  As she simmered and fried,
"I'm damned if I don't—or I do."
George Libaire

Way of the Transgressors

There was an old fellow of Lynn
Who had never committed a sin,
   But when the old Pharisee
   Went over to Paris, he
Said, "It's never too late to begin."

A book and a jug and a dame,
And a nice cozy nook for the same;
  "And I don't care a damn,"
  Said Omar Khayyam,
"What you say, it's a great little game."

There was an old monk of Siberia
Whose life it got drearier and drearier.
  He escaped from his cell,
  With a hell of a yell,
And eloped with the Mother Superior.

There was an old Fellow of Trinity,
A doctor well versed in Divinity;
  But he took to free-thinking,
  And then to deep drinking,
And so had to leave the vicinity.

◇◇◇◇

Said old Peeping Tom of Fort Lee:
"Peeping ain't what it's cracked up to be;
  I lose all my sleep,
  And I peep and I peep,
And I find 'em all peeping at me."
                                Morris Bishop

◇◇◇◇

A rheumatic old man in White Plains,
Who will never stay in when it rains,
   Has a home full of drugs
   Kept in little brown jugs—
And that's all he gets for his pains.

Barnyard and Bird Sanctuary

The cautious collapsible cow
Gives milk by the sweat of her brow;
   Then under the trees
   She folds her front knees
And sinks fore and aft with a bow.

There was an old man of Khartoum
Who kept two tame sheep in his room.
"For," said he, "they remind me
Of one left behind me,
But I cannot remember of whom."

There was a young lady of Venice
Who used hard-boiled eggs to play tennis:
When they said, "You are wrong,"
She replied, "Go along!
You don't know how prolific my hen is."

A cannibal bold of Penzance
Ate an uncle and two of his aunts,
   A cow and her calf,
   An ox and a half,
And now he can't button his pants.

A wonderful bird is the Pelican;
His bill can hold more than his belly can.
   He can hold in his beak
   Enough food for a week,
And I wonder how in the hell he can.

This bird is the Keel-billed Toucan,
Whose size doesn't do what his hue can,
   His color scheme rates
   A succession of dates,
Which consist of just settin' and lookin'." [9]
               Howard Ketcham

Music Hath Charms

There was an Old Person of Tring
Who, when somebody asked her to sing,
   Replied, "Aren't it odd?
   I can never tell 'God
Save the Weasel' from 'Pop Goes the King.'"

There was a young fellow named Hatch
Who was fond of the music of Bach.
   He said: "It's not fussy
   Like Brahms and Debussy.
Sit down, and I'll play you a snatch."

A lieutenant who went out to shoot
Some Riffiians, holding a butte,
   Felt exceedingly queer,
   When impaled by a spear.
For that was the Riff in the Lieut.
Morgan Taylor

There was a young lady at Bingham
Who knew many songs and could sing 'em;
But she couldn't mend hose
And wouldn't wash clothes,
Or help her old mother to wring 'em.

There once was a popular crooner
Who was anything else but a tuner;
But he crooned once too often,
Now he's snug in his coffin,
And I wish he had landed there sooner.
                    M. B. Thornton

Said the Reverend Jabez McCotton,
"The waltz of the Devil's begotten."
  Said Jones to Miss Bligh,
  "Never mind the old guy,
To the pure almost everything's rotten."
James Montgomery Flagg

Travelers by Land and Sea

There was a young man of Ostend
Who vowed he'd hold out to the end;
  But when half-way over
  From Calais to Dover,
He done what he didn't intend.

There was a young woman named Bright,
Whose speed was much faster than light,
   She set out one day
   In a relative way,
And returned on the previous night.

—◇◇◇—

There was a young man who said, "Damn!
It is borne upon me that I am
   An engine that moves
   In predestinate grooves.
I'm not even a bus; I'm a tram."

—◇◇◇—

There was a young lady of Twickenham,
Whose shoes were too tight to walk quick in 'em;
   She came back from her walk,
   Looking white as a chalk,
And took 'em both off and was sick in 'em.

Oliver Herford

◇◇◇

A silly young fellow named Hyde
In a funeral procession was spied;
   When asked, "Who is dead?"
   He giggled and said,
"I don't know; I just came for the ride."

◇◇◇

There was a young man who said, "Run,
For the end of the world has begun."
   And his audience ran
   All the way to Milan,
Without ever discharging a gun.

Words, Words, Words

A flea and a fly in a flue
Were caught, so what could they do?
   Said the fly, "Let us flee."
   "Let us fly," said the flea,
So they flew through a flaw in the flu ..

There once was a man of Calcutta
Who spoke with a terrible stutta.
   At breakfast he said,
   "Give me b - b - b - bread
And b - b - b - b - b - b - butta."

There was a young lady of Woosester
Who usest to crow like a roosester
   She usest to climb
   Two trees at a time,
But her sisester usest to boosest her.

A tutor who tooted a flute
Tried to teach two young tooters to toot;
  Said the two to the tutor,
  "Is it harder to toot, or
To tutor two tooters to toot?"
                        Carolyn Wells

When a jolly young fisher named Fisher
Went fishing for fish in a fissure,
  A fish, with a grin,
  Pulled the fisherman in.
Now they're fishing the fissure for Fisher.

A canner remarkably canny
Remarked one day to his granny,
  "A canner can can
  Anything that he can,
But a canner can't can a can, can he?"

Our Gallery of Art

There once was a sculptor called Phidias
About whom I won't be invidious,
   But he carved Aphrodite
   Without any nightie,
Which shocked all the pure and fastidious.
                Oliver Herford

A nice old lady named Tweedle
Went to church and sat down on a needle.
  Though deeply imbedded,
  'Twas luckily threaded,
And was deftly pulled out by the beadle.[10]

A wonderful family is Stein;
There's Gert and there's Ep, and there's Ein
  Gert's verses are punk,
  Ep's statues are junk,
And nobody understands Ein.

There was a young maid who said, "Why,
Can't I look in my ear with my eye?
  If I give my mind to it,
  I'm sure I can do it,
You never can tell till you try." [11]

For Whom the Bell Tolls

There was a young fellow named Sydney.
Who drank till he ruined his kidney.
  It shriveled and shrank,
  As he sat there and drank,
But he'd a good time doin' it, did'ney?
Don Marquis

A certain young gourmet of Crediton
Took some *pâté de foie gras* and spread it on
  A chocolate biscuit,
  Then murmured, "I'll risk it."
His tomb bears the date that he said it on.

There was a Young Lady of Niger
Who smiled and rode out on a Tiger.
  They returned from the ride
  With the Lady inside,
And the smile on the face of the Tiger.

Yes, theirs was a love that was tidal,
And it ended in cheer that was bridal
But the bridegroom said, "Dear,
Let's, please, have some beer."
And they buried them seidel by seidel.
Paul Kieffer

There was a young lady of Byde
Who ate a green apple and died;
The apple fermented
Inside the lamented,
And made cider inside her inside.

All young men should take note of the case
Where the guy necked his gal at its base.
   No, the gal did not choke,
   But her vertebra broke,
And that was her final embrace.

                    M. B. Thornton

He died in attempting to swallow,
Which proves that, though fat, he was hollow—
   For in gasping for space,
   He swallowed his face,
And hadn't the courage to follow.[12]

                    Roy Campbell

Oxford Don's Book of Verse

God's plan made a hopeful beginning
But man spoiled his chances by sinning.
  We trust that the story
  Will end in God's glory,
But, at present, the other side's winning.

O God, inasmuch as without Thee,
We are not enabled to doubt Thee,
    Pray grant of Thy grace
    That the whole human race
May know nothing whatever about Thee.

Evangelical vicar in want
Of a portable second-hand font,
    Will give for the same
    A photo (in frame)
Of the Bishop-elect of Vermont.
                Ronald Arbuthnott Knox

There was an old fellow of Trinity
Who solved the square root of Infinity,
　　But it gave him such fidgets
　　To count up the digits
That he chucked Math and took up Divinity.

<><><>

There was a young man who said, "God,
It ever has struck me as odd
　　That the sycamore tree
　　Simply ceases to be,
When there's no one about in the quad."

<><><>

"Dear Sir: Your astonishment's odd.
I am always about in the quad;
    And that's why the tree
    Still continues to be,
Since observed by Yours faithfully, God."

Dress Parade

There was a young belle of Old Natchez,
Whose garments were all shreds and patches;
　　When comment arose
　　On the state of her clothes
She drawled, "When Ah itches, Ah scratches." [18]

There was an old man of the Cape
Who made himself garments of crêpe;
    When asked, "Will they tear?"
    He replied, "Here and there,
But they keep such a beautiful shape." [14]

◇◇◇◇

"The styles that at present are regnant,"
She wrote, "seem to favor the pregnant
    I'm told they are swell
    (And you know I can't spell)
But I think they are simply repegnant."

◇◇◇◇

There was a young man from Quebec
Who sat in snow up to his neck.
　　When asked, "Are you friz?"
　　He said, "Yes, I is,
But we don't call this cold in Quebec." [15]

Our Own Noah's Ark
(or The Birds and the Beasts Were There)

A certain young fellow, named Bobbie
Rode his steed back and forth in the lobby:
    When the clerk said: "In doors
    Is no place for a horse"
He replied: "But, you see, it's my hobby."

There was a young man of Hong Kong
Who invented a topical song.
 It wasn't the words
 That bothered the birds,
But the horrible double ontong.[16]

◇◇◇

A Clergyman out in Dumont
Keeps a tropical fish in the font;
 Though it always surprises
 The babes he baptizes,
It seems to be just what they want.
Morris Bishop

◇◇◇

Said a great Congregational preacher
To a Hen, "You're a beautiful creature."
    And the Hen, just for that,
    Laid an egg in his hat;
And thus did the Hen reward Beecher.[17]

The Bucket Brigade

There was an old man of Nantucket
Who kept all his cash in a bucket;
   But his daughter, named Nan,
   Ran away with a man,
And as for the bucket, Nantucket.
          Princeton Tiger

Pa followed the pair to Pawtucket
(The man and the girl with the bucket)
  And he said to the man,
  "You're welcome to Nan."
But as for the bucket, Pawtucket.

Chicago Tribune

Then the pair followed Pa to Manhasset,
Where he still held the cash as an asset:
  And Nan and the man,
  Stole the money and ran,
And as for the bucket, Manhasset.

New York Press

There once was a man who said, "How
Shall I manage to carry my cow?
  For if I should ask it
  To get in my basket,
'Twould make such a terrible row." [18]

The Poet and the Gasman [19]
(or *Nothing in Excess*)

There was a young man from Japan
Who wrote verses no one could scan:
    When they told him 'twas so,
    He replied, "Yes, I know,
But I like to get as many words in the last line as I can."

A decrepit old gasman, named Peter,
While hunting around for the meter,
　　Touched a leak with his light;
　　He rose out of sight—
And, as every one who knows anything about poetry
　　can tell you, he also ruined the meter.

Department of Sanitation—1864 [20]

There was a gay damsel of Lynn
Whose waist was so charmingly thin,
   The dressmaker needed
   A microscope—she did—
To fit this slim person of Lynn.

There was a dear lady of Eden,
Who on apples was quite fond of feedin';
 She gave one to Adam,
 Who said, "Thank you, Madam."
And then both skedaddled from Eden.

There was an old man who said, "Do
Tell me how I'm to add two and two?
 I am not very sure
 That it doesn't make four,
But I fear that is almost too few."

There once was a person of Benin,
Who wore clothes not fit to be seen in;
   When told that he shouldn't,
   He replied, "Gumscrumrudent,"
A word of inscrutable meanin'.

Relativity and Levitation

I wish that my Room had a Floor,
I don't so much care for a Door,
But this walking around
Without touching the ground,
Is getting to be quite a bore!

Gellett Burgess

There once was a girl of New York
Whose body was lighter than cork;
　　She had to be fed
　　For six weeks upon lead
Before she went out for a walk.
　　　　　　　Cosmo Monkhouse

As a beauty, I am not a star.
There are others more handsome, by far.
　　But my face, I don't mind it,
　　For I am behind it.
It's the people in front get the jar.[21]
　　　　　　　Anthony Euer

You remember that pastoral frolic
(It now seems oddly symbolic)
   When the moon was the hurdle
   Though the milk it might curdle
And give all the babies the colic.
R. K. B.

Legion Etrangère[22]
("Vers Nonsensiques"—quoted by Carolyn Wells)

A Potsdam les totaux absteneurs
Comme toutes d'autres titotalleurs,
   Sont gloutons omnivores,
   Nasorubicolores,
Grands machons, et terribles duffeurs.

Un vieux duc (le meilleur des époux)
Demandait (en lui tâtant le pouls)
  A sa vielle duchesse
  (Qu'un vieux catarrhe oppresse)
"Et ton thé, t'a-t-il ôté la toux?"

Il naquit près de Choisy-le-Roi,
Le Latin lui causait de l'effroi,
  Et les Mathématiques
  Lui donnaient de coliques,
Et le Grec l'enrhumait. Ce fût moi.

Il était un gendarme à Nanteuil
Qui n'avait qu'une dent et qu'un œil,
   Mais cet œil solitaire
   Etait plein de mystère,
Cette dent, d'importance et d'orgueil.
            George du Maurier

Il y avait une jeune fille de Tours,
Un peu vive, qui portait toujours
   Un chapeau billy-coque,
   Un manteau peau-de-phoque,
Et des p'tits pantalons au velours.

Un Marin naufragé (de Doncastre)
Pour prière au milieu du désastre,
   Répétait au genoux
   Ces mots simple et doux
"Scintillez, scintillez, petit astre!"
      George du Maurier

Il était un jeune homme de Dijon
Qui se moquait de toute religion;
   Il disait une fois
   "Moi, je m'en fiche des trois,
Le Père, et le Fils, et le Pigeon."

Aristophanes Improved

The limerick presented to Aristophanes appears in a book entitled *Greek Social Life*, by F. A. Wright. In the last act (to call it so) of *The Wasps* sundry characters are taking part in a symposium, or get-together for drinks, topical songs, and snatches. The spirit of many of these snatches is the spirit of the limerick—of that there is no manner of doubt—but the limerick form is lacking. Other translators have tried to preserve the Greek form in the English version—and missed the spirit. But not Mr. Wright. And this is what he has made of one sample:

> An amateur, driving too fast,
> From his car to the roadway was cast:
>   And a friend kindly said,
>   As he bandaged his head,
> "Mr. Cobbler, stick to your last."

The translator adds that though the tipple of these roistering Athenians was only wine, "copiously diluted with water," the company rarely dispersed till daylight.

Picked Up at the Mermaid

William Shakespeare's contribution to this polite anthology was discovered by E. W. Boyer, of Earleville, Maryland, and is found in *Othello*, Act II, Scene 3. Iago, to gain his private ends, is plying Cassio with liquor. The tough old Top-Sergeant sings a song which (he says) he picked up in England, where "they are most potent in potting." This is it:

> And let the canakin clink, [clink]
> And let the canakin clink,
> A soldier's a man;
> And life's but a span,
> Why, then, let the soldier drink.

The Bard, you may note, has done a fairly orthodox job—though the repeated line is the second and not the fifth as in Lear. We may assume, I think, that the extra "clink" is a stage direction. The date of the play is 1604. Thus we have contemporary testimony that limericks were sung by Britons in pot-houses nearly two hundred and fifty years before Lear made nonsense of them.

Elizabeth R. Fecit

Moving up quite a bit in the social scale, Leonard Bacon will have it that Shakespeare's Royal Patron, Queen Elizabeth, who, likewise, upon occasion wooed the muse, *almost* made a limerick. You will find it in The Oxford Book of English Verse, and it runs thus:

> The daughter of debate
> Who discord aye doth sow,
>   Hath reaped no gain
>   Where former reign
> Hath taught still peace to grow.

As we look at it, the Royal Hand has bid the anapest go hang. But *La Reine le veult*. And, besides, says Bacon—a proved poet in his own right—strict enforcement of the anapestic rule is unfair to limericks. At Yale, he remembers, they used the paeonic measure.[23]

106

W. S. Gilbert's Compliments to E. Lear[24]

Sir W. S. Gilbert, who, as we have seen, dropped into limericks—perhaps unconsciously—in turning Oscar Wilde into the game of "Patience," took a fall out of Lear in what he called "A Nonsense Rhyme in Blank Verse." The very Learical sample beginning, "There was an Old Man in a Tree, Who was horribly bored by a Bee," became in the Gilbertian version:

> There was a young man of St. Bees
> Who was stung in the arm by a wasp.
> When they asked, "Does it hurt?"
> He replied, "No, it doesn't,
> But I thought all the time 'twas a hornet."

As you might expect, Sir William, while he discarded rhymes, did not let the anapests miss a beat. And, by the way, this heterodox confection has been credited by patriotic Irishmen to George Bernard Shaw.

In Friendship's Name
(*or Love Among the Artists*) [25]

There is a young artist named Whistler
Who in every respect is a bristler;
   A tube of white lead
   Or a punch in the head,
Come equally handy to Whistler.
              Dante Gabriel Rossetti

There is a creator named God
Whose doings are sometimes quite odd,
  He made a painter named Val,
  And I say—and I shall—
That he does no great credit to God.
                    J. M. Whistler

Thinking Makes It So

A limerick packs laughs anatomical
Into space that is quite economical.
  But the good ones I've seen,
  So seldom are clean,
And the clean ones so seldom are comical.

Your verses, dear friend, I surmise
Were not meant for clerical eyes:
   The Vicar and Dean
   Cannot tell what they mean,
And the Bishop's aghast with surprise.

Envoi

(With Apologies to Oliver Herford)
and The Players

In this book every line has been clean;
Not a word that's profane or obscene,
　　Or spelled in four letters
　　That might pain our betters,
Or snafu—if you know what we mean.

Notes

[1] Acknowledgments and apologies to Pooh-Bah, Lord High Everything Else.

[2] See also Sir W. S. Gilbert's version.

[3] One of the rare Lear examples in which the lazy line is *not* used.

[4] In the paeonic measure preferred at Yale.

[5] Just remember that Salisbury used to be spelled Sarum, and taking all the obstacles in this course is easy.

[6] Harlow S. Pearson, of Tree Top, Southern Pines, North Carolina, calls this a "choice example of the limericks whose rhymes depend upon abbreviations."

[7] It has been pointed out that the epicure did not dine at Crewe by choice—he was caught there changing trains between Oxford and Cambridge.

[8] Quoted by Langford Reed in *The Limerick Book*.

[9] Howard Ketcham, of 101 Park Avenue, New York, in calling attention to this one, remarked: "A veritable trade mark of color engineering—yellow, red, blue, black, and white—is Tux the Toucan."

[10] Though neglected now in the best families, needle work is still a fine art.

[11] Modern Art can turn this trick without trying.

[12] This unfortunate gentleman is identified by the author as Polybius Jubb.

[13] *De minimis non curat lex.*

[14] Louis Untermeyer in *The Holiday Reader* says Robert Louis Stevenson wrote this one.

[15] Snow-clad—as in mountains. Untermeyer gives this one to Rudyard Kipling.

[16] In another version the birds are of the feathered variety. Perhaps you prefer it. We chose this one.

[17] Attributed by Untermeyer to Oliver Wendell Holmes.

[18] The basket is introduced into this famous New England-Long Island symphony because we did not have another bucket handy. Compare this limerick to the Lear original from which it was derived:

> There was an Old Man who said, "How
> Shall I flee from this horrible Cow?
>   I will sit on the stile
>   And continue to smile,
> Which may soften the heart of this Cow."

[19] These two have been called limericks-to-end-all-limericks.

[20] Quoted by Carolyn Wells from books printed for the New York Fair for the benefit of the Sanitary Commission, 1864. The Fair was not for street cleaners, by the way, but for wounded and sick soldiers of the Civil War. The first two are clearly period pieces, and follow the Lear pattern, with a last line as lazy as any of his.

[21] This, we have been many times told, was the favorite of President Woodrow Wilson. It appeared first in the *Princeton Tiger*.

[22] Though only two are signed, the author of *Trilby* is probably responsible for most of these French confections.

[23] For the benefit of the curious with a taste for erudition Mr. Bacon supplies this:

"It appears to me, after what I consider a happy flash of recollection, that the limerick is a specialized form of what used to be called, according to Saintsbury, Poulter's Measure. One line contains a dozen syllables and the next fourteen, and both were dear to the hearts of Wyatt and Surrey, the first poets in modern English. Queen Elizabeth is writing Poulter's Measure in this

stanza, but she made the first step toward the formation of a limerick by introducing the interior rhyme in
the fourteen-syllable line. The next step is to introduce
an interior rhyme at the end of the third foot of the
twelve-syllable line, when the measure may be said to
be born."

[24] It has also been pointed out that the spirit of the
limerick is not absent from the *Bab Ballads*. There is
even a pretty close approach to the form. Take this
from "The Story of Prince Agib."

> Of Agib, who amid Tartaric scenes,
> Wrote a lot of ballet music in his teens:
>   His gentle spirit rolls
>   In the melody of souls—
> Which is pretty, but I don't know what it means.

The presence of some extra short syllables will distress
the purists, of course, and they may emit short, sharp
barks of grief and rage. But, certainly, the spirit of the
limerick is on the job, let the feet fall where they may.

[25] These limericks follow the pattern set by Lear—
lazy line and all. "The Blessed Damozel" was written
only a few years after *The Book of Nonsense* came out,

and though Whistler's fame arrived later, more non-sense books by Lear continued to appear. We have here the proof that serious—and even supercilious—artists, his contemporaries, found that the plaything the nursery rhymester had promoted came in handy as a weapon of offense.

Reserved for Your Favorite Limericks

Reserved for Your Favorite Limericks

Reserved for Your Favorite Limericks